Pathway to Grammar

Student's Book

5

Richmond

Richmond
58 St Aldates
Oxford
OX1 1ST
United Kingdom

Pathway to Grammar Student's Book Level 5

First Edition: 2015
Seventh Reprint: 2023
ISBN:978-607-06-1096-7

Publisher: Justine Piekarowicz
Editorial Team: Jennifer S. Li, Joep van der Werff
Art and Design Coordinator: Marisela Pérez
Design: Erika Martínez
Layout: Paola Romero
Pre-Press Coordinator: Daniel Santillán
Pre-Press Team: Susana Alcántara, Virginia Arroyo
Cover Design: Erika Martínez

Cover Photograph: ©**THINKSTOCK:** iStock (harlanov, EpicStockMedia); Hemera (Cathy Yeulet); Polka Dot (Jupiterimages)

Illustrations: Erick Arellano pp. 6, 28, 48; Sheila Cabeza de Vaca pp. 8, 10, 25, 46, 69; Sebastian Hernández p. 38; Luis Montiel pp. 5, 9, 19, 21, 26, 35, 47, 57, 60, 67, 76, 79; Alma Nuñez pp. 7, 11, 29, 45, 68, 70; Ismael Vázquez p. 80; Carlos Vélez pp. 17, 39, 40, 55, 59, 77; David Yañez pp. 15, 18, 37, 58, 61, 75, 78

Photographs: ©**REPOSITORIO:** Ediciones Santillana, S.A. (Argentina) p. 50; Ediciones Santillana, S.A. (España) pp. 10 (José María Escudero Ramos, José Vicente Resino Ramos), 37 (MUSEUM ICONOGRAFÍA), 64 (Sergio Antonio Enríquez Nistal); Editora Moderna, Ltda. p. 31; Richmond Publishing S.A. de C.V. (México) p. 52 (Elias Hermann Salas Martínez);©**THINKSTOCK:** AbleStock.com p. 47 (Hemera Technologies); Blend Images pp. 16 (Stewart Cohen/ Jensen Walker), 24 (JGI/Jamie Grill), 28 (Inti St Clair), 34 (John Lund/Sam Diephuis) 53 (John Lund); Creatas pp. 15 (Jupiterimages), 19 (Jupiterimages), 24 (Jupiterimages), 34 (Creatas Images), 43 (Jupiterimages), 44 (Creatas Images), 64 (Creatas Images), 74 (Creatas Images); Digital Vision pp. 12 (Martin Poole), 14 (Tay Jnr), 20 (Digital Vision), 27 (Digital Vision),35 (Anup Shah), 46 (Tom Le Goff), 54 (Siri Stafford), 64 (Max Oppenheim), 74 (James Woodson); Eyecandy Images p. 19 (Eyecandy Images); FogStock p. 82 (FogStock/Vico Images/Marv Johnson); Getty Images News p. 68 (Sean Gallup); Hemera pp. 4 (Anton Starikov), 9 (Jose manuel Gelpi diaz, Serghei Velusceac), 10 (Roman Sigaev), 19 (Edyta Linek), 28 (John Mcallister), 38 (Konstantin Grishin), 44 (Glen Jones), 54 (Boris Ryzhkov), 71 (Henrik Lehnerer), 73 (Murat Keles), 76 (Aidar Ayazbayev); iStock pp. 3-83 (Ociacia), 4 (kreinick, McIninch, K_attapon, daboost, Vladimir Nikitin, VladZymovin, dimdimich, olgakr, scanrail, Givaga, yang yu, Mimadeo), 6 (Serp77, chargerv8, de santis paolo), 7 (Elena Schweitzer, Ljupco, AlexStepanov, Diana Taliun, belchonock, Vichly44), 8 (design56, scanrail, boojedsada, Dieter Meyrl, Eric Hood), 9 (SLP_London, Preto_perola, rgbdigital, sweetok, yelo34, antpkr, sunstock, photka), 10 (smontgom65, dramaj, sceka, Daniel Sanchez Blasco, belchonock, 3Dmask), 12 (Korovin, borabalbey, TKphotography64, Brenda A. Carson, macbrianmun, truembie, ClaxtonPhotography), 13 (KovacsAlex, fotocelia), 14 (KovacsAlex, JannHuizenga, Igor Kovalenko, luanateutzi, YanLev, jodiejohnson, Magnascan, Evgeny Karandaev, José María Bouza Valverde, Tomwang112), 15 (SERGEY BELOV, DariaZu), 16 (travnikovstudio, Zhenikeyev, mg7, vinicef, luminouslens), 19 (borisovv, Todd Gunkel, Gennadiy Kondratyev), 20 (Kirschner, Ryhor Bruyeu, franck camhi), 22 (chas53, JackF), 23 (EduardHarkonen, Ben Blankenburg, frontpoint), 24 (marcduf, Lana_Stem, Vadmary, ShooteRhys, axelbueckert, Jonathan Austin Daniels, pialhovik), 25 (Michelle Milliman, ClaudioVentrella), 27 (Tomwang112, rvbox, RebeccaHarris2014, harlanov), 28 (nyul, nataka, Astrid Gast, luismmolina), 30 (StockRocket, scanrail, Robert Churchill, Oleksiy Mark, uatp2, tarasov_vl, margouillatphotos, Kareivis, Leonid Andronov, Osuleo, tiler84), 32 (Grassetto, BrianAJackson, MaryTMoore, monkeybusinessimages), 33 (Maksym Bondarchuk, AlinaMD), 34 (AntonioGuillem, Grata Victoria, AlexandrMoroz, vicspacewalker, audioundwerbung, Toa55, LeeJianbing), 35 (ginosphotos, littlestocker, IPGGutenbergUKLtd), 36 (Dmitrijs Dmitrijevs, shironosov, Marek Slusarczyk, AlinaMD, kokoroyuki), 37 (VvoeVale), 38 (kvasay, Corey Ford), 39 (Alexander Podshivalov, WesAbrams), 41 (sv-time, Allevinatis), 42 (egal, Mckyartstudio, stokkete), 43 (kali9, diego_cervo, RV72, mikemcd), 44 (Oliver Helbig, AndreyPopov, MR1805, starmaro, Pinkypills, OlgaMiltsova, Harvepino, Catherine Yeulet, Julenochek, 3dan3), 46 (Antonio_ Diaz, Alliance, fabthi, poligonchik), 47 (Tracy Fox, chat9780, JackF), 49 (IPGGutenbergUKLtd, Ljupco, ginosphotos), 50 (berpin), 51 (Slanapotam, pay404), 53 (Studio-Annika, SergiyN, magda_rzymanek), 54 (Robert Churchill, Devonyu, SZE FEI WONG, Siuzanna Fonarova, rsester, Peter Zijlstra, belchonock, g-stockstudio, CARLOSVOSS), 55 (anna1311, AnjelaGr, macgyverhh), 56 (JackF, gpointstudio), 57 (scanrail, monkeybusinessimages, Chalabala), 58 (david franklin, sprng23, Chalabala, Tomasz Gierygowski, PaulMichaelHughes), 59 (spetnitskaya nadya, GooDween123, silatip, Valentyn Volkov, vinicef), 62 (ivan_baranov, cao chunhai, ClaudioVentrella, Ievgeniia Lytvynovych, XiXinXing), 63 (ISerg, lucato, Christophe Testi, Mariusz Blach, simonkr), 64 (1971yes, Maxim Petrichuk, odmeyer, luvemakphoto, LeventKonuk, JoseIgnacioSoto, IPGGutenbergUKLtd, Jon Gorr, cdoughboy2000, evgenyatamanenko, VladimirFLoyd, christingasner), 65 (JuNi Art, serezniy, ventdusud, Lucky_Guy, MatteoCozzi, SlidePix), 66 (IPGGutenbergUKLtd, Nicole S. Young, Alexander Novikov, fotokostic, Julien Lemarchand), 67 (photochecker, pius99, EccentricCanvas, Adrian Lindley), 68 (elenasendler), 71 (Okea, tatajantra, kevin mayer, dimdimich, VVCephei), 72 (mocker_bat, Sera⊠na, xalanx), 73 (GooDween123, Jacek Chabraszewski, gbh007), 74 (gongzstudio, Ljupco, Piotr Adamowicz, Andrew Johnson, vencavolrab, Stefani_Ecknig, decisiveimages, Aneese, ginosphotos, Balazs Kovacs, Toni Scott), 76 (-Dant-, koto_feja, Johan Swanepoel, changered, Sashkinw), 77 (mg7, monkeybusinessimages, Pawel Gaul, Neostock), 79 (Galina Barskaya), 81 (monkeybusinessimages), 82 (viki2win, 123ArtistImages), 83 (fergregory, Roman_Gorielov, rmnunes, kasto80, Baloncici), 84 (unalozmen), 85 (Gennadiy Kondratyev), 86 (Anne-Louise Quarfoth), 89 (szefei), 90 (Suze777), 91 (Taalvi); iStock Editorial pp. 32 (nito100), 41 (sihasakprachum), 48 (mjbs), 54 (xyno); liquidlibrary p. 38 (Jupiterimages, Dynamic Graphics,2007); Monkey Business p. 52 (Monkey Business Images Ltd); moodboard pp. 15 (moodboard, Mike Watson Images), 42 (moodboard), 44 (moodboard), 55 (moodboard), 58 (moodboard), 66 (moodboard); Photodisc pp. 20 (Martin Poole), 24 (Digital Vision), 27 (Medioimages/Photodisc), 28 (Sky View), 34 (Photodisc, Ryan McVay), 36 (David De Lossy), 44 (Digital Vision), 57 (David De Lossy), 63 (Ryan McVay), 74 (Photodisc), 85 (Leonard Mc Lane); PhotoObjects.net p. 4 (Hemera Technologies); Photos.com pp. 14 (Jupiterimages), 36 (Photos.com), 37 (Photos.com), 74 (Photos.com); Pixland p. 30 (Jupiterimages); Stockbyte pp. 4 (George Doyle), 13 (Stockbyte), 24 (Jupiterimages), 44 (Jupiterimages), 55 (Stockbyte), 66 (Brand X Pictures), 76 (Brand X Pictures), 79 (George Doyle); TongRo Images p. 44 (TongRo Images); Top Photo Group pp. 34 (Top Photo Corporation), 46 (Top Photo Corporation); Valueline p. 19 (Photodisc); Wavebreak Media pp. 13 (Wavebreakmedia Ltd), 16 (Wavebreakmedia Ltd), 49 (Wavebreakmedia Ltd); Zoonar pp. 24 (Zoonar RF), 57 (Zoonar RF), 74 (Zoonar RF); pp. 14 (Purestock), 15 (Fuse), 19 (Ingram Publishing), 23 (Purestock), 24 (Fuse, Ingram Publishing), 27 (David Spurdens/www.ExtremeSportsPhoto.com/Fuse), 33 (Fuse), 34 (Purestock, Fuse), 41 (Dorling Kindersley), 42 (Ivary), 45 (Fuse), 49 (Fuse), 54 (Fuse), 59 (Howard Shooter), 64 (Fuse), 66 (Ingram Publishing), 82 (Fuse, Purestock)

Printed in Brazil by Forma Certa Gráfica Digital
Lote: 808136
Codigo: 292710967 / 2025

Contents

Unit 1

backpack

heavy (*adj*)

pitcher

scissors

screen

1 shelf, 2 shelves

telephone, phone

tools

Materials

cloth

glass

gold

metal

paper

plastic

silver

wood

Conjunctions *and, but, or*

1 Read and circle the correct picture.

1. David likes chocolate and vanilla ice cream.

2. Sarah Jane wears sunglasses or a hat every day.

2 Look and match.

1 

2 

3 

1	You can wear the green dress,	but	then he dried them.
2	She likes going shopping,	and	you can wear the red dress.
3	He washed our clothes	or	she doesn't like spending money.

G

Passive voice in present, affirmative

1

F

active voice = I build the house.
passive voice = The house **is built** (by someone).

1 Choose, color, and write.

1 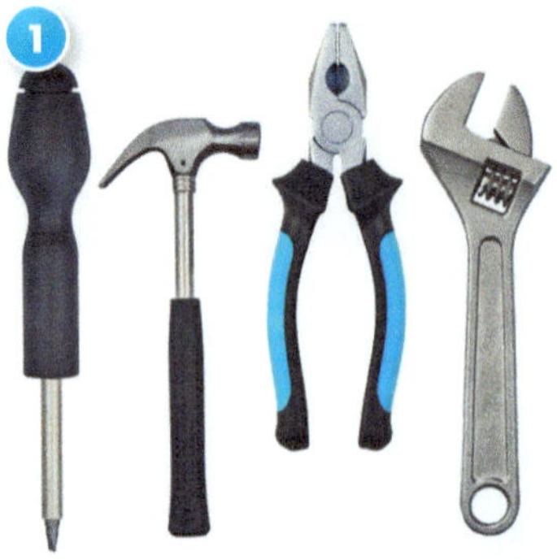

2 

3 

4 

1 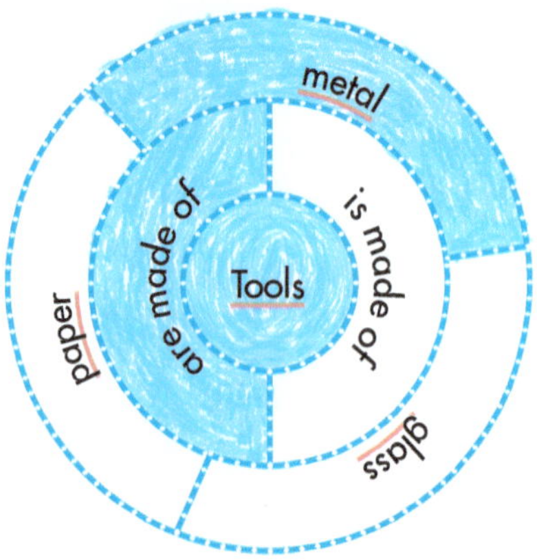

Tools are made of metal.

2 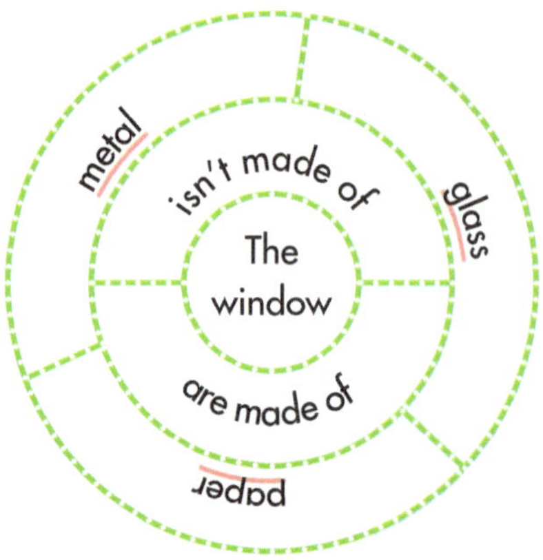

____.

3 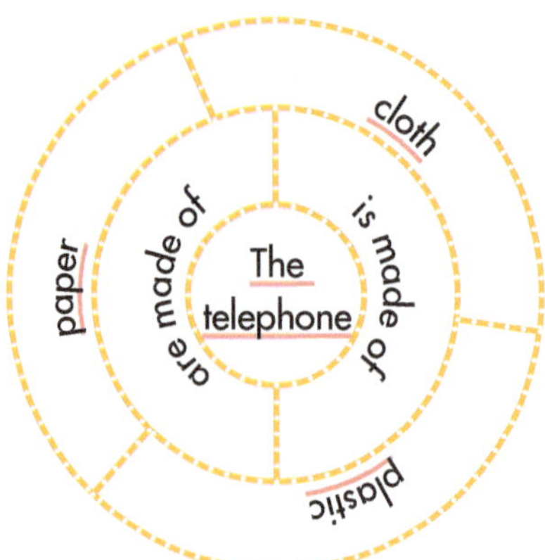

____.

4 

____.

Passive voice, negative

1 Match and write.

The sweaters | are made of | plastic. | glass. | The bowl | isn't made of

aren't made of | They | cloth. | It | is made of | metal.

1. *The sweaters aren't made of plastic*.
   They ______________________.
2. *The bowl* ______________________.
   ______________________.

2 Look, read, and circle *T* (True) or *F* (False).

1. The tea set is made of wood. T (F)
2. The bowl and spoon are made of glass. T F
3. The pitcher is made of silver. T F
4. The mirror is made of gold. T F

3 Rewrite the false sentences. Use *isn't* or *aren't*.

The tea set isn't made of wood. The ______________________

____

Conjunctions with affirmative and negative

1 Look, read, and write.

1 

2 

3 

4 

5 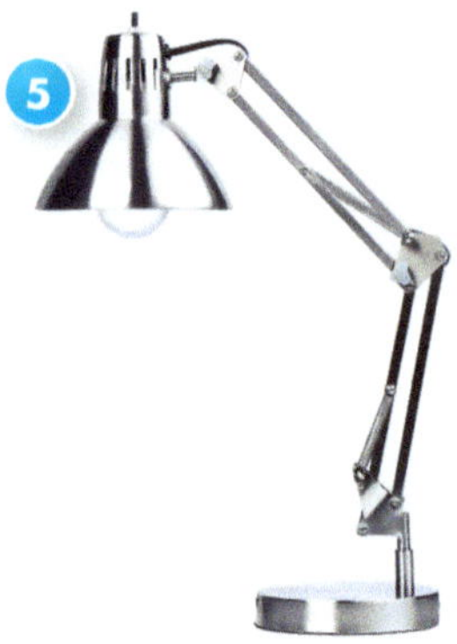

1. (*cloth*, *plastic*) The *backpack* *is made of cloth and plastic*.
2. (*gold*, *silver*) The *screen* isn't ____.
3. (*wood*, *metal*) The guitar ____.
4. (*wood*, *glass*) The robot ____.
5. (*metal*, *glass*) The lamp ____.

2 Draw an object and write about it.

1. It's made of __________ and __________.
2. It isn't made of __________ or __________.

Passive voice with *What...?*

1 Look and write.

glass metal paper plastic wood

1 

2 

3 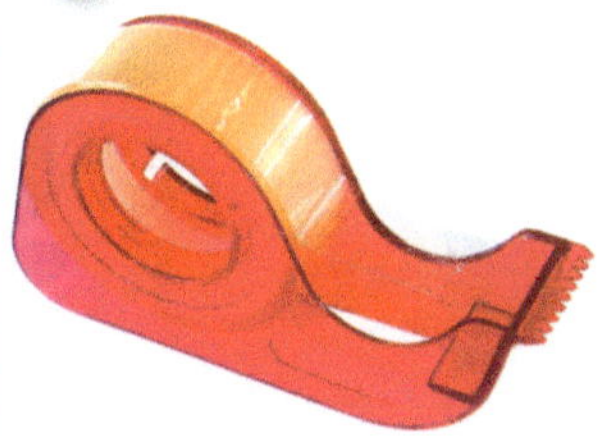

4 

5 

1. *What are they made of*? *They're made of metal*.
2. *What is it* ____________? *It's* ____________.
3. ____________? ____________.
4. ____________? ____________.
5. ____________? ____________.

2 Look, read, and circle.

1. What ***are*** / ***is*** scissors made of?
   They're made of plastic ***and*** / ***or*** metal.

2. What ***are*** / ***is*** bags made of?
   They're made of paper ***and*** / ***or*** plastic.

1 **Look and write.**

✓ permitted ✗ forbidden

1. Fishing is forbidden.
2. Food and drinks are __________.
3. Fires are __________.
4. Camping is __________.

2 **Look again and write.**

1. Is fishing permitted? No, it isn't.
2. Are food and drinks allowed? __________.
3. Are fires forbidden? __________.
4. Is camping permitted? __________.

3 **Look and write.**

accepted allowed forbidden permitted

1. Is glass accepted? Yes, it is.
2. Are plastic bottles __________? __________.
3. __________? __________.
4. __________? __________.

4 Look, unscramble, and answer.

1. permitted / here / parking / is

   Is parking permitted here?

   Yes, it is.

2. cell phones / are / forbidden / on / plane / the

   ______________________________?

   ______________.

3. here / accepted / credit cards / are

   ______________________________?

   ______________.

4. adults / in / tree house / this / are / allowed

   ______________________________?

   ______________.

5. is / sold / ice cream / here

   ______________________________?

   ______________.

6. allowed / on / ride / short / the / children / are

   ______________________________?

   ______________.

1 Listen and write. 2

aren't they | doesn't it | isn't it | is she

HARRY: That box is heavy, ___isn't it___?

EMMA: Yes, it is! Can you help me pick it up?

HARRY: Sure! It goes in the kitchen, ____________?

EMMA: Yes, but let's be careful. The box is made of paper, and there are heavy plates inside!

HARRY: It's okay. The plates are made of plastic, ____________?

EMMA: No, they aren't!

HARRY: Oops.

EMMA: Oh, no! All the plates are broken!

HARRY: Mom isn't going to be happy about this, ____________?

EMMA: No, she isn't!

2 Read the dialogue with a friend.

3 Talk with a friend. Then write.

Adjectives: interesting | pretty | ugly | unusual

Materials: cloth | metal | plastic | wood

A: Look! This is ____________ (adjective), isn't it?

B: Yes, it is. It's made of ____________ (material), isn't it?

A: These are made of ____________ (material), too.

B: They're ____________ (adjective), aren't they?

A: Yes, they are!

Let's sing!

1 Listen and write. Then draw. 3

The Empty Room

bright

desk

leather (*adj*)

vase

1. Look at this room.
There's nothing at all.
Listen to this rap.
Imagine and draw.

2. There is a vase
On a square table.
It's as green as grass
And it's made of glass.

3. There is a desk
Next to the table.
This desk is fantastic
'Cause it's made of plastic.

4. There is a lamp
That's very bright.
It's good for all weather
And it's made of leather.

5. Look at this room
It's not empty at all.
Only you're not there.
Draw your picture
anywhere!

Unit 2

Adjectives

bright

dark

hard soft

foggy

large

low

noisy

tidy

warm

borrow (*v*)

lend (*v*)

boil (*v*)

ice (cubes) (*n*)

shorts (*n*)

sky (*n*)

Zero conditional 4

1 Match and write. Then number.

1 

2 

3 

4 

5 

6 

☐	If you cut an onion,	he runs in circles.
☐	If we watch a horror movie,	you make orange.
1	If you mix red and yellow paint,	they get sunburned.
☐	If the dog is happy and excited,	you cry.
☐	If people don't wear sunscreen,	you get a parking ticket.
☐	If you don't park your car correctly,	we scream.

1. *If you mix red and yellow paint, you make orange*.
2. ______________________________.
3. ______________________________.
4. ______________________________.
5. ______________________________.
6. ______________________________.

2 Look and complete.

boil burn do well get colder miss the train

1. If students think a lot before answering questions on a test, they do well.

2. If you leave cookies in the oven too long, ______________________________.

3. If you put ice in your lemonade, ______________________________.

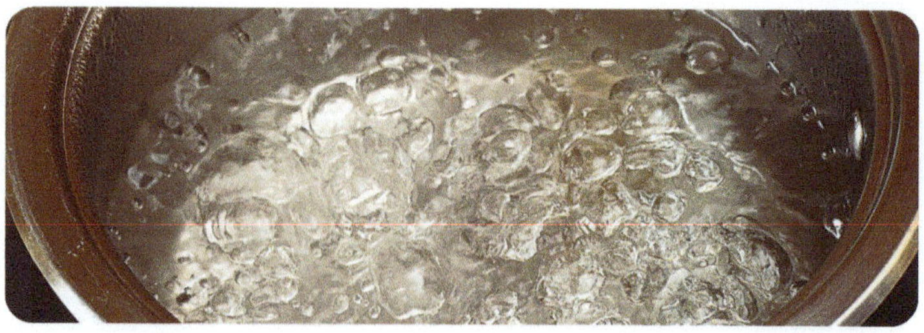

4. If water reaches 100 degrees Celsius, ______________________________.

5. If you don't check the times carefully, ______________________________.

Problem verbs

1 Sort. Use the *Grammar Summary*.

an activity | your bed | chores | a decision | dinner | homework | laundry | a mistake | a phone call | a puzzle

Make	Do
____________	*an activity*
____________	____________
____________	____________
____________	____________
____________	____________

2 Look, read, and label. Use the *Grammar Summary* on page 85.

1. *Earn or win?*

earn

win

2. *Borrow or lend?*

____

____

3. *Know or meet?*

____

____

4. *Lose or miss?*

____

____

3 **Look, read, and write. Use the *Grammar Summary* on page 85.**

1 know / meet

William ___knows___ two movie stars. He ___met___ them at the gym.

2 miss / lose

Yesterday James ________________ his passport and ________________ his flight!

3 earn / win

I can't ________________ any money, but maybe I can ________________ the lottery.

4 make / do

George always ________________ all his homework, but he ________________ a lot of mistakes.

5 borrow / lend

Last week, I ________________ my best friend my sweater, and I ________________ her jacket.

Too, not...enough

1 Look and circle.

1 

2 

3 

4 

1. His shoes are ***too big*** (circled) / ***not large enough***.
2. Her sunglasses are ***too small*** / ***not small enough***.
3. His jacket is ***too long*** / ***not big enough***.
4. His hat is ***too low*** / ***not low enough***.

2 Look and write.

1 

2 

3 

4 

1. (*tidy, messy*) His room is too messy. It isn't tidy enough.
2. (*short, tall*) The girl is too short. She's ______________________.
3. (*quiet, noisy*) The drums are ______________________.
4. (*heavy, light*) Her suitcase is ______________________.

3 Look, read, and match.

1 
2 
3 
4 

The sky is clear and dark. | It's warm and sunny. | It rains. | It's foggy and there's ice on the road.

We wear shorts and sunglasses. | He observes the stars. | People don't drive. | I don't play soccer.

4 Look again and write. Use *if*.

1. *If it rains, I don't play soccer*.
2. ______________________.
3. ______________________.
4. ______________________.

5 Unscramble.

1. soft / is / too / this / pillow
   This pillow is too soft.
2. that / isn't / blanket / enough / warm
   ______________________.
3. room / dark / the / isn't / enough
   ______________________.
4. too / lights / bright / are / the
   ______________________.
5. enough / outside / quiet / isn't / it
   ______________________.

6 Draw and write about yourself.

1. *If the weather is sunny, I* ______________________________.
2. ______________________________.
3. ______________________________.
4. ______________________________.
5. ______________________________.
6. ______________________________.
7. ______________________________.
8. ______________________________.
9. ______________________________.
10. ______________________________.

1 Listen and write. 5

first finally next then

MOM: Would you like to learn how to make peanut butter cookies?

MIKE: Yes, I would! What should I do first?

MOM: __First__, mix a cup of peanut butter, a cup of sugar, a teaspoon of vanilla, and an egg in a bowl.

DAD: ________, drop spoonfuls of the mixture onto a baking sheet.

MOM: If you use a fork to make cross marks, the cookies look pretty.

DAD: ________, bake the cookies for ten minutes.

MOM: Be careful. If you bake cookies too long, they burn!

DAD: ________, let the cookies cool.

MOM: If cookies don't have time to cool, they get too soft.

MIKE: Thanks, Mom and Dad! These cookies are delicious!

2 Read the dialogue with two friends.

3 Talk with a friend. Then write.

A: Here's how to make scrambled eggs.

B: First, ____.

A: Next, ____.

B: Then, ____.

A: Finally, ____.

B: Fry the eggs on low heat until they're done.

A: Then, enjoy your scrambled eggs!

Let's sing!

1 Listen, read and write. 6

board   helmet   life jacket   raft

boring   exciting   frightening   fun   scared

Extreme Sports

Do you want to go snowboarding today?
If you do, get your ____________ and follow me.
Put your ____________ on and balance.
Let yourself go and fly through the air.

Do you feel the spray of snow on your face?
Don't let the snow beat you.

Chorus:
Extreme sports, extreme sports
I'd like to do them all.
They're ____________; I'm ____________.
They're ____________ and ____________.
They're not ____________ at all!

Do you want to go whitewater rafting today?
If you do, get your ____________ and follow me.
Put your ____________ on. We're off!
Take your seat and paddle down the rapids.

Do you feel the spray of water on your face?
Don't let the speed beat you.

(Chorus)

2 Now answer the questions.

If you want to go snowboarding, you need *a (snow)board and* ____________

____________.

If you want to go whitewater rafting, you need ____________

____________.

How do you feel if you do an extreme sport?

If I ____________, I feel ____________.

Unit 3

begin – began (*v*)

finish (*v*)

cartoon (*n*)

century (*n*)

collect (*v*)

destroy (*v*)

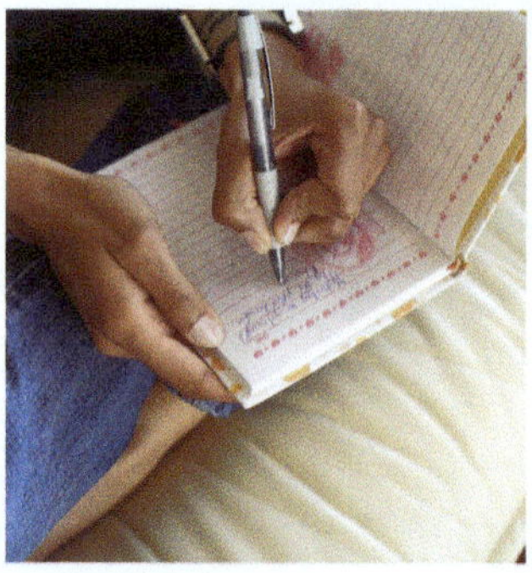

diary (*n*)

lie – lay (*v*)

lose – lost (*v*)

find – found (*v*)

online (*adv*)

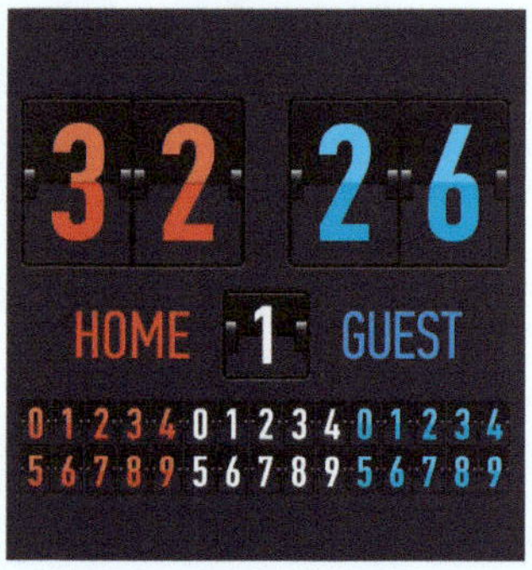

score (*n*)

suitcase (*n*)

surf (*v*)

wave (*n*)

winner (*n*)

Simple past, affirmative

regular verbs in past: base verb + *ed*
irregular verbs in past: irregular forms

1 Match.

be   eat   get   play

rain   stay   take   watch

ate   got   played   rained

stayed   took   was / were   watched

2 Look again, read, and write the past forms.

Dear Diary,
Yesterday it *rained*, so my big sister and I __________ inside. First, we __________ breakfast and __________ cartoons on TV. Next, we __________ video games online. I __________ the high score, so I __________ the winner! Then, we __________ tired, so we __________ a nap.

3 Write about and draw yourself.

Dear Diary,
Yesterday was a fun day!
I ______________________________
____
____
______________________________.

4 Number, circle, and write.

1 lie / lose

look / leave

run / ride

find / finish

Last Saturday, William lost his wallet. He ____

____

____.

begin / finish

come / go

build / destroy

make / do

Yesterday Emma ____

____

____.

Simple past, negative 7

I / You / He / She / It / We / They **didn't**...

1 **Look and write. Use *didn't*.**

build a sandcastle | collect seashells | go sailing | lie in the sun | surf

	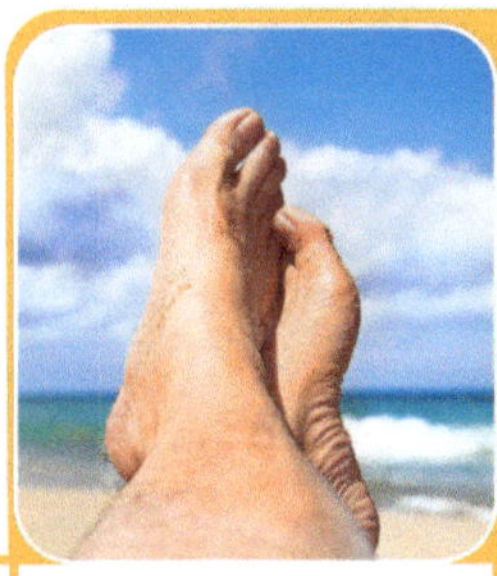				
Adam		✓	✓	✓	
Susan and Sam			✓	✓	✓
My aunt	✓	✓		✓	
My parents	✓	✓			✓
Me	✓		✓		✓

1. Adam didn't lie in the sun, and he didn't surf.
2. ______________________________.
3. ______________________________.
4. ______________________________.
5. ______________________________.

Simple past, interrogative

Did I / you / he / she / it / we / they…

1 Look and write.

1. *buy vegetables*

   Did the man buy vegetables?

   No, he didn't. He bought shoes.

2. *go to the movies*

   _____ the woman ____________________?

   Yes, ____________________.

3. *watch soccer on TV*

   _____ they ____________________?

   ____________________.

4. *ride their bikes*

   _____ the boys ____________________?

   ____________________.

5. *eat her food*

   _____ the dog ____________________?

   ____________________.

6. *climb the tree*

   _____ the cat ____________________?

   ____________________.

1 

2 

3 

4 

5 

6 

2 Answer for yourself. Write complete sentences.

1. Did you go to school yesterday? _____, I ____________________.
2. Did you do exercise yesterday? _____, I ____________________.

Used to, affirmative and negative

I / You / He / She / It / We / They **used to**…
I / You / He / She / It / We / They **didn't use to**…

1 Match.

2 Look again and write.

1. He didn't use to do any exercise. Now he goes to the gym every day.
2. She used to ________________________.
3. ________________________.
4. ________________________.
5. ________________________.

Used to, interrogative

Did I / you / he / she / it / we / they **use to**…

1 Look and write.

eat listen play ride swim watch

Amy:

1. Did you use to swim in a pool?
2. Did you use to ____________________?
3. ____________________?
4. ____________________?
5. ____________________?

Amy's grandmother:

1. No, I didn't. I used to swim in the sea.
2. ____________________.
3. ____________________.
4. ____________________.
5. ____________________.

2 Read and write the simple past forms.

close eat have is listen live ride sail watch wear (2x)

Life in the Middle Ages

The Middle Ages lasted from about the 5th century to the 15th century. This time in history is also called the Dark Ages because very few people could read or write. Only a few had access to culture and education. Life in the Middle Ages ___was___ very different from life today.

In the Middle Ages, very rich people __________ large, beautiful castles, but most people __________ in cold, dark houses. Windows __________ small, and people __________ them at night for security.

People in the Middle Ages didn't travel as much as people today. When they had to travel, they __________ horses or __________ on the sea in large ships.

Clothing was not the same as it is today. People didn't use to wear jeans or tennis shoes. Women __________ long dresses, and men __________ long jackets or tunics. People didn't use to eat hamburgers or pizza. They __________ meat, fish, and vegetables.

There were no movie theaters or TVs. Instead, people __________ to musicians and storytellers. They also __________ the clowns and jugglers that visited their towns and cities.

1

2

3

4

3 Look at the pictures and answer the question.

What did people in the Middle Ages use to do?

1. People used to __________.
2. __________.
3. __________.
4. __________.

1 Listen, write, and label. 8

finally first next then

DAVID: Hi, Holly! How was your vacation?

HOLLY: Hi, David! Spain was beautiful, but I'm glad to be home!

DAVID: Why? What happened?

HOLLY: ___First___, we flew to Madrid. The flight was great. But the airline lost our suitcases!

DAVID: Oh, no! What did you do next?

HOLLY: __________, we went shopping in the city. We had to buy all new clothes!

DAVID: What happened then?

HOLLY: __________, my dad lost his credit card.

DAVID: Did he find it?

HOLLY: No, he didn't! __________, we went to Bilbao to see the Guggenheim Museum.

DAVID: That place is amazing, isn't it?

HOLLY: I don't know. On the day we went, it was closed!

____

___First___

____

____

2 Read the dialogue with a friend.

3 Talk with a friend. Then write.

eat go (shopping, swimming,...) play read see sleep watch

A: What did you do last weekend?

B: First, I ______________________________.

A: What did you do next?

B: Next, ______________________________.

A: And then what did you do?

B: Then, ______________________________.

A: What did you do after that?

B: Finally, ______________________________.

Did you practice with the Pathway to Certification app?

Let's sing!

1 Listen and write the verbs. 9

be	go	keep	know	need (2x)	play	see (2x)	watch

My Lady

Chorus:
Where __________ you __________, my lady?
Why _____are_____ you so far from me?
When can I __________ you, my lady?
You __________ I __________ you,
I __________ you with me!

I __________ a million games,
I __________ a thousand miles,
I __________ a hundred faces,
Just to __________ you smile!

(Chorus)

Not the highest mountain,
Not the biggest sea,
Not the longest river,
Can ________ you from me!

Unit 4

across (*prep*)

over (*prep*)

past (*prep*)

through (*prep*)

up (*prep*) down (*prep*)

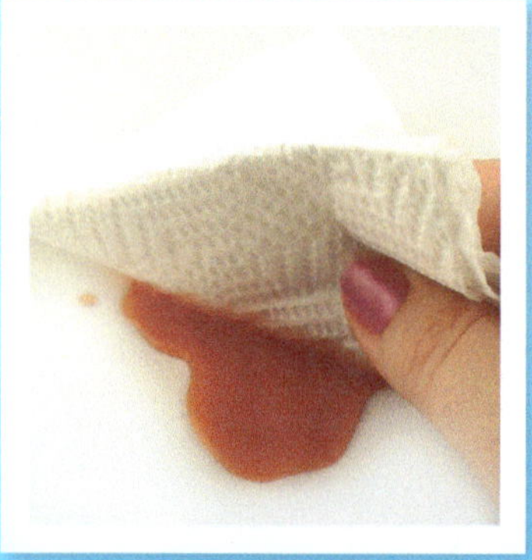
absorb (*v*)

air (*n*)

bronze (*adj*)

cave (*n*)

direct (*v*)

discover (*v*)

evaporate (*v*)

invent (*v*)

path (*n*)

stadium (*n*)

Prepositions of movement 10

1 Read, look, and number.

1

1. The businessman is falling **onto** the floor.
2. The man is moving **past** the bus.
3. The balloon is flying **over** the ocean.
4. The animals are going **across** the river.

2 Follow and write.

1

2

3

along

down

into

through

toward

up

4

5

6

1. The robot is moving ___along___ the path.
2. It's flying ____________ the gold ring.
3. It's crashing ____________ the wall.
4. It's ____________________ the goal.
5. It's ____________________ the rope.
6. It's ____________________ the hill.

Passive voice in present

regular verbs: is / are invented, found by...
irregular verbs: is / are grown, given by...

1 Read and rewrite in passive voice.

1. Rivers carry water to oceans and lakes.
   Water is carried to oceans and lakes by rivers.
2. The sun evaporates the water.
   ______________________________.
3. The water forms clouds in the air.
   ______________________________.
4. Rain and snow return the water to the ground.
   ______________________________.
5. The ground absorbs the water again.
   ______________________________.

Passive voice in past, affirmative

regular verbs: **was / were discovered**, **built** by…
irregular verbs: **was / were stolen**, **broken** by…

1 Match and write.

Mona Lisa

Shakespeare

Bell

1. The play *Hamlet*	direct	Alexander Graham Bell
2. The song *Yesterday*	name after	Paul McCartney
3. The *Mona Lisa*	invent	Amerigo Vespucci
4. The telephone	paint	Leonardo da Vinci
5. America	sing	Steven Spielberg
6. *A.I.* and *E.T.*	write	William Shakespeare

1. *The play Hamlet was written by William Shakespeare* around 1600!
2. ____,
who also wrote the music and the lyrics.
3. ____
500 years ago!
4. ____,
who also was a teacher of the deaf.
5. ____,
an Italian explorer.
6. The movies ____.

1 Look and write.

1. *In 776 B.C. the first ancient Olympic Games were held by the Greeks*.
2. In 1896 ______________________________.
3. In 1848 ______________________________.
4. In 1912 ______________________________.
5. In 1879 ______________________________.
6. In 1961 ______________________________.

2 Read and write.

break	destroy	rob	steal	turn

Officer Jones talked to the owner of the store.
Here's what she found out:

1. The store *was robbed*.
2. The windows ______________________.
3. The door ______________________.
4. The alarm ______________________ off.
5. All the money ______________ by the robbers.

Passive voice, interrogative

1 Read, write, and number.

Finding the *Atocha*

The *Atocha* was a Spanish treasure ship that sank in 1622. The Spanish government searched for the ship for 70 years before they gave up.
The ship remained lost for the next 363 years. But in 1985, the treasure was found by Mel Fisher and his crew. The *Atocha* was discovered 40 miles west of Key West, Florida.
Fisher spent $15 million on equipment to make his expedition successful. He even created a special machine. It was named the *Mailbox*. The machine produced a current of clear water so the divers could see the sea floor.
Forty-seven tons of silver and jewels were found on the *Atocha*, and 150,000 gold coins and bars were recovered. The treasure filled two entire museums that Fisher built to display his discovery.

build	create	discover	find	lose	name	recover	spend

1. How long _was_ the *Atocha* _lost_?
2. When ____ the ship _discovered_?
3. How much ____________ on equipment?
4. Where ____ the *Atocha* ________?
5. How many gold coins and bars ________?
6. Why ____ a special machine ________?
7. What ____ the machine ________?
8. How many museums ________ by Fisher?

- [ ] To help divers see the sea floor.
- [ ] Near Key West, Florida.
- [ ] The *Mailbox*.
- [ ] In 1985.
- [1] Three hundred sixty-three years.
- [ ] Two.
- [ ] Fifteen million dollars.
- [ ] One hundred fifty thousand.

2 Read and draw.

Treasure Map

First, climb over the mountain and walk past the trees. Then, go toward the lake and swim across it. Next, jump over the quicksand. Finally, walk toward the cave, and go into it. You'll find the treasure under a red rock.

3 Draw and write. Use at least six of the prepositions.

across along down into onto over past through toward up

My Treasure Map

How to Find the Treasure

____
____
____
____
____
____
____
____

What the Treasure Is

____

____________________ *was* / *were* hidden here!

4 Read, circle, and write.

A History of the Olympics

The Ancient Olympic Games

The ancient Olympic Games ***was*** / ***were*** __________ (*play*) around 776 B.C. in Greece.

Foot races, wrestling, boxing, the pentathlon, and chariot races were among the sports included in the first Olympic Games. Only men ***was*** / ***were*** ____________________ (*permit*) to take part in them.

After that, the ancient Olympic Games took place every four years until 393 A.D., when they ***was*** / ***were*** ____________________ (*forbid*) by Emperor Theodosius.

The Modern Olympic Games

The modern Olympic Games ***was*** / ***were*** __________ (*hold*) in Athens in 1896. Now, the summer and winter Olympic Games ***are*** / ***is*** __________ (*hold*) every four years in different cities around the world.

Beautiful stadiums ***are*** / ***is*** __________ (*build*) to house the competitions. Tickets ***are*** / ***is*** __________ (*sold*) so people can watch the events. Gold, silver, and bronze medals ***are*** / ***is*** __________ (*give*) to the top athletes.

5 Unscramble and answer.

1. the ancient Olympic Games / first / where / held
   Where were the ancient Olympic Games first held? *In Greece*.
2. permitted / to take part / in the ancient Olympics / who / was
   ____? ____________________.
3. when / the ancient Olympic Games / forbidden / were
   ____? ____________________.
4. the modern Olympic Games / hold / were / when
   ____? ____________________.
5. is / to the winners / in the modern Olympics / what / given
   ____? ____________________.
6. held / the summer and winter Olympics / are / how often
   ____? ____________________.

1 Listen and write. 11

DANNY: Wow, I can't believe we're finally at the ___Olympics___!

SARAH: Yes, but I think we're late!
Excuse me, what time does the opening ___________ start?

GUIDE: It starts at ___________. You'd better hurry!

SARAH: Sorry, what time? Could you say that again, please?

GUIDE: _______________________.

DANNY: Can you tell us how to get there?

GUIDE: Go ___________ this path ___________ the stadium.
Walk ___________ the gate and ___________ the stairs.
Then, just show the guards your tickets.

DANNY: Thank you!

GUIDE: Have a great time at the ___________!

2 Read the dialogue with a friend.

3 Talk with a friend. Then write. Use some of the prepositions.

across along down into onto over past through toward up

At the movie theater

A: What time does ________ start?

B: It starts at ___________ in theater ______.

A: Can you tell me how to get to theater _____?

B: Go ______________________________
______________________________.

A: Sorry, could you say that again, please?

B: Yes! Go ___________________________
______________________________.

A: Thank you!

Let's sing!

1 Listen and write the prepositions. 12

at	down	of	on	in	to	under	up	with

Summer Camp

Last week I went __________ the lake.
I camped __________ the stars,
And played __________ a snake.
I hiked __________ the mountain,
And painted a fountain, ooh!

Chorus:
It's because I went __________ summer camp,
Summer camp, playing __________ the sun.
Summer camp, summer camp:
Games, friends, and lots __________ fun.
Summer camp, summer camp,
I went __________ summer camp.

I sailed __________ a boat __________ sea.
I walked __________ and __________ the beach,
And climbed __________ a great palm tree.
I surfed __________ really big waves,
And visited some interesting caves, ooh!

(Chorus)

Summer camp, summer camp,
Summer camp, playing __________ the sun.
Summer camp, summer camp:
Games, friends, and lots __________ fun.
Summer camp, summer camp,
I went __________ summer camp!

Unit 5

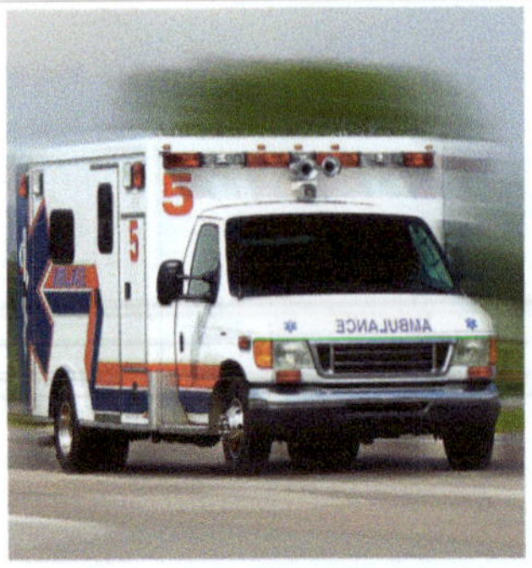

ambulance

bridge

brush your teeth (*v*)

1 tooth, 2 teeth

cut (*n*, *v*)

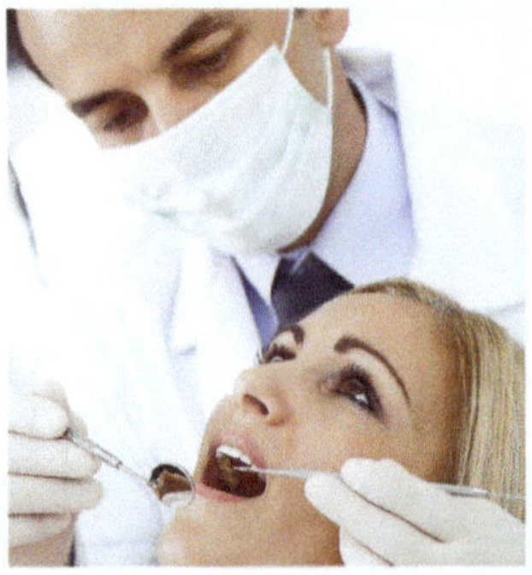

dentist

dinosaur

extinct (*adj*)

fossil

fall down, fell down (*v*)

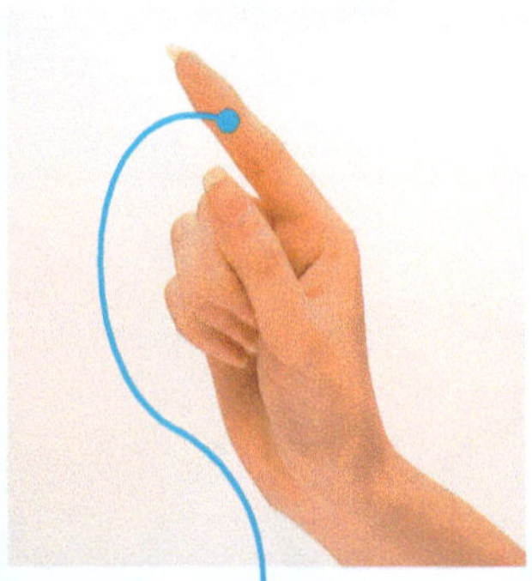

finger

hurt (*v*)

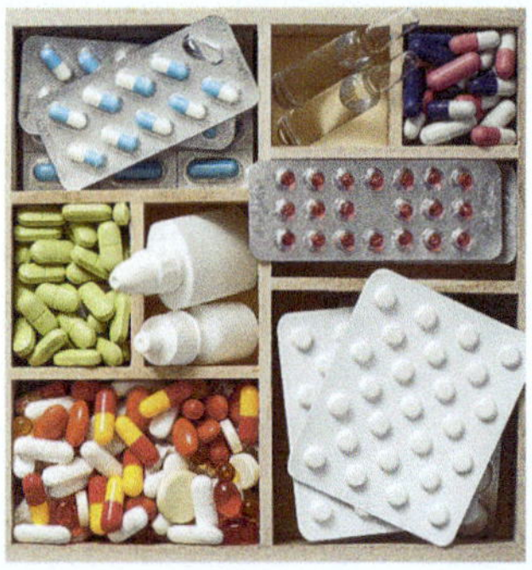

medicine

planet

race (*n*, *v*)

toe

traffic

First conditional, affirmative 13

If it's hot outside, I'll wear shorts.
(condition) (result)

1 Look and write.

rain snow sunny windy

fly a kite go swimming play cards ski

1  *If it's windy, we'll fly a kite*.

2  *If it rains,* ______________________.

3  ______________________
______________________.

4  But ______________________
______________________!

2 Follow and write.

1. I
2. He
3. She
4. They

the countryside
the lake
the city
the mountains

go fishing and swimming.
walk in the fields.
ski in the snow.
eat at good restaurants.

1. *If I go to the city, I'll eat at good restaurants*.
2. ______________________.
3. ______________________.
4. ______________________.

First conditional, negative

If it isn't hot outside, I won't wear shorts.
(condition) (result)

1 Match the conditions and results.

Conditions	Results
1. I don't fix the car.	She doesn't feel better.
2. You don't use the knife carefully.	You get a toothache.
3. Sue doesn't take medicine.	The car doesn't start.
4. People throw trash on the ground.	The streets aren't clean.
5. You don't brush your teeth.	You cut your finger.

2 Look again, number, and write.

1. If I don't fix the car, it won't start.
2. ______________________.
3. ______________________.
4. ______________________.
5. ______________________.

First conditional with *unless*

I won't wear shorts **unless** it's hot outside.
(result) (condition)

1 Look and write.

be call feel go has take

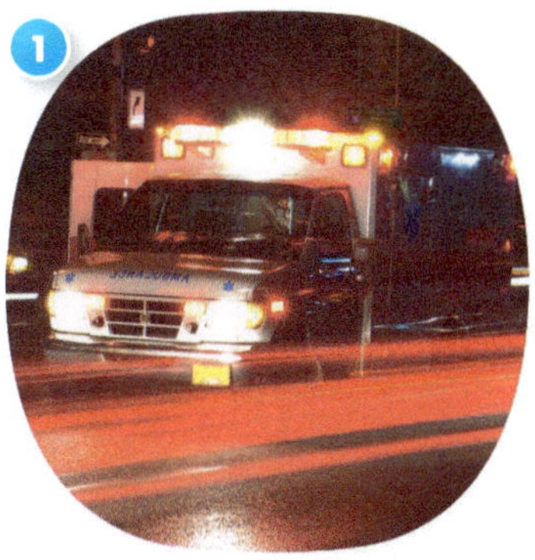

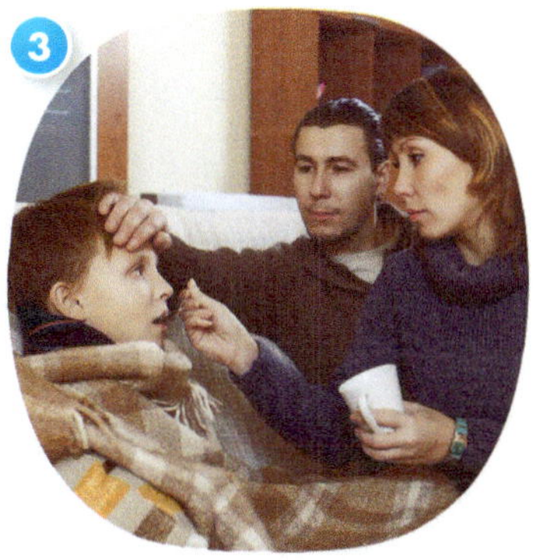
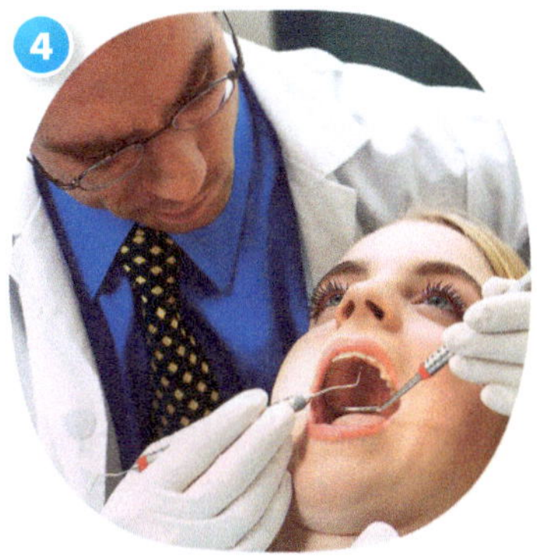

1. They __won't call__ an ambulance __unless it's__ an emergency.
2. I ______________ late ______________________ a lot of traffic on the road.
3. Alex ______________ medicine ______________________ very ill.
4. Emily ______________ to the dentist ______________________ a toothache.

2 Look, write, and draw.

1. He won't stop crying unless ______________
______________________________.

2. We won't go on vacation unless ______________
______________________________.

Need to, affirmative

1 Read the article. Then, write and mark T (*True*) or F (*False*).

Running a Marathon

The legend says that on a hot summer's day in 490 B.C., a Greek soldier named Philippedes ran 26 miles from Marathon to Athens to deliver the news about the defeat of the Persians. Totally exhausted, he died after the good news reached the city.

In honor of Philippides's run, marathons are run all over the world, including during the Olympic Games. The race is 26.2 miles, or 42 kilometers, long.

Because of the long distance, marathon runners work hard for many months to prepare for a race. It's important for athletes to eat healthy food and to exercise regularly. Their training should include lifting weights at the gym. It's also important to have good shoes and run in them often before a race.

Preparing for a marathon takes time, but athletes still continue to work or study and relax with friends. Rest days are important for the body. And after all, a good state of mind is as important as physical fitness, especially in the last miles of a race!

buy eat exercise include rest stop

1. You *need to eat* a lot of sugar when preparing for a marathon.	T	(F)
2. You ______________ expensive new shoes right before the race.	T	F
3. You ______________ on some days, for your body and your mind.	T	F
4. You ______________ regularly when preparing for a race.	T	F
5. You ______________ both running and lifting weights in your training.	T	F
6. You ______________ studying, working, and having friends.	T	F

Need to, negative

1 Circle the odd one and write.

ride a bike	helmet	kneepads	flashlight

1. You don't need to have a flashlight to ride a bike.

become a dentist	be tall	study hard	love to work

2. ______________________________.

play basketball	tennis shoes	bat	net

3. ______________________________.

go to the beach	coat	swimsuit	sunblock

4. ______________________________.

drive	driver's license	a lot of money	car

5. ______________________________.

2 Read. Then unscramble and circle.

Digging Up the Past

Dinosaurs are animals that lived on this planet millions of years ago. Today they are extinct, but they once lived everywhere.

Scientists believe that a large rock called a meteorite hit the Earth, probably causing these creatures to become extinct.

Approximately two hundred years ago, people began finding dinosaur fossils. The first fossils were discovered in England.

Looking for fossils is not an easy task, but many more things need to be done once scientists have found a dinosaur fossil.

Fossil Q&A

1. to / what / scientists / do / need / first / do

   What do scientists need to do first?

   They need to remove the rocks from around the bones to…

   (a.) look for the fossils. b. make a campfire.

2. how / clean / need / do / scientists / to / the bones

   ______________________________?

   They need to clean the bones by…

   a. breaking them. b. brushing them.

3. scientists / number / the bones / why / to / need / do

   ______________________________?

   They need to number the bones to…

   a. put the skeleton together. b. play a memory game.

4. the skeleton / to / take / to a museum / need / do / scientists / why

   ______________________________?

   They need to take the skeleton to a museum to…

   a. bury it in the ground again. b. allow people to see it.

3 Read and match.

Mike's Horoscope for Today

Don't ride your skateboard today, or you'll fall down and have an accident.

You need to wear a sweater while playing outdoors, or you'll catch a cold.

An old friend will probably call you. You need to listen to him carefully! You'll find out something very interesting.

Your mom won't be in a very good mood today, so do your homework and behave yourself.

Your dog may not be feeling very well. You may need to take him to the vet.

1. If Mike rides his skateboard,
2. If Mike plays without a sweater,
3. If a friend calls Mike,
4. If Mike does his homework,
5. If Mike's dog feels ill,

- he'll need to take him to the vet.
- his mom will be happy.
- he'll fall down and have an accident.
- he'll get some important information.
- he'll catch a cold.

4 Read and circle T (*True*) or F (*False*).

Superstition Trivia

Do you know common superstitions?

1. If you don't blow out all the candles on your birthday cake, your wish will come true.	T	(F)
2. If you say good-bye to a friend on a bridge, you'll see each other again.	T	F
3. If a bee enters your home, you'll have visitors.	T	F
4. If you count the seeds in an apple, you'll know how many children you'll have.	T	F
5. If you break a mirror, you won't have seven years of bad luck.	T	F

Answers: 1. F, 2. F, 3. T, 4. T, 5. F

5 Check your answers. Then correct the false sentences.

If you don't blow out all the candles on your birthday cake, your wish won't come true.

______________________________.

______________________________.

Let's talk!

1 Listen and write. 14

NURSE: Good morning, City __Hospital__. How can I help you?

PATIENT: I think I need to ________________ right away!

NURSE: What's the matter?

PATIENT: Well, I didn't ____________________ last night.

NURSE: If you have a __________, you'll need to see a ______, not a ______.

PATIENT: No, I don't have a __________.

NURSE: What's the matter, then?

PATIENT: It's my ______ and my ______. I got out of bed to __________. It was dark, so I didn't see a ______ on the floor. I fell down and hurt my ______. I cut my ______, too!

NURSE: Okay. I don't think we need to send an __________, but you need to see the ______ in his office. I'll tell him you're coming.

PATIENT: Thank you! Good-bye.

NURSE: Good-bye.

2 Read the dialogue with a friend.

3 Talk with a friend. Then write.

Body Parts

finger head neck
stomach tooth toe

Actions

drink eat rest
see a doctor take medicine

A: What's the matter?

B: My ____________ hurts.
(body part)

A: What happened?

B: ____
____.

A: You need to ________________________________.
(treatment)

B: Okay. I'll try that. Thanks!

Did you practice with the Pathway to Certification app?

Let's sing!

1 **Complete the lyrics with verbs in the past. Then listen and check.** 15

When I Was a Little Kid

Chorus:

When I was a little kid, I *didn't do* (*not do*) a lot of things.
How *could* (*can*) I be such a fool?
When I was a little kid, I __________ (*not do*) a lot of things.
What a waste of time!

I __________ (*not like*) to eat fish then.
My mom __________ (*try*) and __________ (*try*) for hours.
I didn't __________ (*not like*) to eat fish then.
But I __________ (*keep*) my mouth closed tight!
(Chorus)

I __________ (*not like*) to dance at all.
I only __________ (*watch*) kids having fun.
I __________ (*not like*) to dance at all,
All by myself drinking juice!
(Chorus)

I ________________ (*not ride*) my bike to the park.
I ________________ (*not play*) with other kids.
I ________________ (*not ride*) my bike to the park,
So I ________________ (*watch*) TV and got fat!
(Chorus)

2 **Now write four sentences with *used to / didn't use to.***

I didn't use to eat fish.

____.

Unit 6

airport

butter

check

chopsticks

dessert

fork knife spoon

ride (*n*)

salt pepper

striped (*adj*) spotted (*adj*)

sugar

taste (*v*)

taxi stand

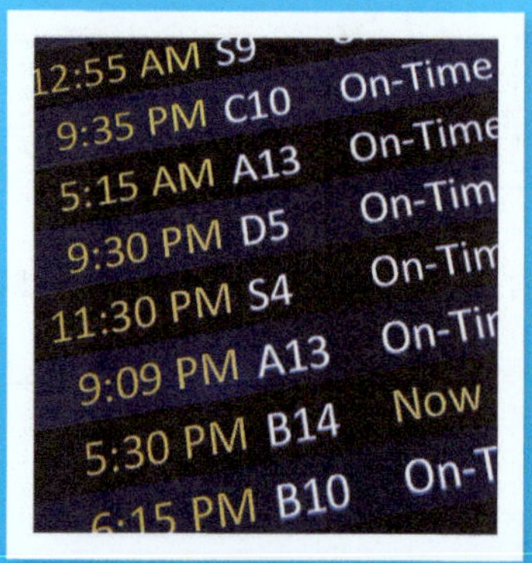

timetable

Offers with *would* 16

What would you like to eat? I'll have the chicken, please.

1 Read, write, and number.

☐ CLIENT: Yes, please, a glass of ice water with lemon.

☐ CLIENT: No, thanks. Just the check after dinner, please.

☐ SERVER: And what would you like to order for dinner?

☐ CLIENT: I'll have the fish with vegetables.

☐ SERVER: After that, would you like some dessert?

1 SERVER: Good evening, sir. Would you like something to drink?

2 Look and write the questions.

butter check chopsticks sugar

1. *Would you like chopsticks* or a fork, knife, and spoon?
2. ______________________ for your tea?
3. ______________________ for your bread?
4. ______________________?

Requests with *could*

1 Read and write.

bring check give try on

1. I don't like the striped dress. *Could you bring me* ______ a spotted one?
2. The orange dress is too small. *Could I* ______ a dress in a larger size?
3. There isn't a price tag on that dress. ______ the price for me?
4. That price is too expensive! ______ a discount?

2 Unscramble. Then read and circle.

Request	Where would you hear it?	
1. I / a single room / have / could / please *Could I have a single room, please* ______?	a. a library	b. (a hotel)
2. explain / could / to me / the timetable / you ______?	a. a train station	b. a toy store
3. with / me / you / help / could / my suitcase ______?	a. an airport	b. a school
4. please / have / two tickets / we / could ______?	a. a school	b. a theater
5. to the airport / give / could / a ride / you / me ______?	a. a supermarket	b. a taxi stand
6. the modern art / is / you / could / tell / me / where ______?	a. a museum	b. a park

Present perfect, affirmative with *already*

1 Follow and write. Use *already*.

1. *I've already checked the timetable at the airport*.
2. *Peter and Kelly have* ______________________________.
3. ______________________________.
4. ______________________________.
5. ______________________________.

2 Look again and number.

☐ 

☐ 

1 

☐ 

☐ 

Present perfect, negative with *yet*

1 Read, look, and write.

It's Mom's day out! Please do the following chores today before 7 o'clock. Love, Mom

Mark and Alex – do your homework	*Dad – clean the office*
Pam and Ann – wash the dishes	*Grandma – cook dinner*
Mike – feed the dog	*Grandpa – iron the clothes*

1. Mark and Alex haven't done their homework yet.
2. Dad hasn't ______________________.
3. ______________________.
4. ______________________.
5. ______________________.
6. ______________________.

2 Write about yourself.

It's almost __________ o'clock, and I haven't ______________________ yet.

Present perfect, interrogative with *yet*

1 **Look and write.**

butter	chocolate	eggs	flour	oil	sugar

Recipe Card: Chocolate Cake

1. (*add*) Have you added the flour yet? — No, not yet.
2. (*break*) ______________________ into the bowl yet? — Yes, I have.
3. (*put*) ______________________? — ______________.
4. (*mix*) ______________________? — ______________.
5. (*pour*) ______________________? — ______________.

2 **Read, look, and write.**

1. Has the chef baked the cake in the oven yet?

   No, not yet.
2. Has she added the chocolate yet?

   ______________________.
3. Has she poured the ingredients into the cake pan?

   ______________________.
4. Have people tasted the cake yet?

   ______________________.

3 Read, look, and write. Use *already* and *yet*.

Jim's Bucket List
(things I want to do in life)

- graduate from college
- win a Nobel Prize
- learn Chinese
- get married
- have two children
- travel to China

1 

2 

3 

4 

1. Has Jim graduated from college yet? Yes, he's already graduated from college.
2. ______________________? ______________________.
3. ______________________? ______________________.
4. ______________________? ______________________.
5. ______________________? ______________________.
6. ______________________? ______________________.

4 Write about and draw yourself.

My Bucket List
(things I want to do in life)

- ______________________
- ______________________
- ______________________

5 Look again and write.

1. Have you ______________ yet? ______________________.
2. Have you ______________? ______________________.
3. ______________________? ______________________.

6 Read, match, and write.

☐ (*drop, bring*)

I've ____________ my fork! Could you ____________ me another one, please?

☐ (*like, try*)

Would you ____________ a fork and knife?

I haven't ____________ the chopsticks yet!

1 (*finish, have*)

I've already *finished* my dinner! Could I ____________ the check, please?

☐ (*taste, add*)

These potatoes ____________ terrible!

You haven't ____________ salt or pepper yet!

☐ (*order, decide*)

Would you like to ____________ dinner?

No, I'm sorry. I haven't ____________ yet!

1 Listen and mark (✓ or ✗). 17

ROSA: Mike, would you like to eat at a restaurant tonight?
MIKE: Sure, Aunt Rosa!
ROSA: Where would you like to go?
MIKE: How about the Argentinian restaurant?
ROSA: I'm sorry. I can't eat a lot of meat. What about the French bakery? They have great desserts!
MIKE: I don't like eating too much sugar. Could we try another place?
ROSA: What about the new Italian restaurant?
MIKE: That's a good idea. I haven't eaten there yet! Could you drive us?
ROSA: Yes, I can. I've already got my car keys!

☐ 

☐ 

☐ 

☐ 

2 Read the dialogue with a friend.

3 Talk with a friend. Then write.

go for a...

drive ride
swim walk

go to a / the...

restaurant mall
soccer game train station

(*A = parent, B = child*)

A: What would you like to do today?
B: Let's go for a ____________.
A: I'm sorry, I can't.
B: That's too bad. Why not?
A: I ______________________________.
How about going to ________________?
B: That sounds great. Could you give me a ride?
A: Yes, I can.
B: Great! Let's do it!

Let's sing!

1 Listen and circle the corresponding pictures. 18

Could You Do Me a Favor?

Chorus:
Could you do me a favor?
Could you, could you,
Could you do me a favor?
Could you do it right now?

Could you pass me that apple?
Could you, could you,
Could you pass me that apple?
Could you pass it right now?

(Chorus)

Could you turn on the TV?
Could you, could you,
Could you turn on the TV?
Could you turn it on now?

(Chorus)

Right now!
Could you do me a favor?
Could you do it right now?
Right now!

2 Write and sing.

Could you ______________________________?
Could you, could you,
Could you ______________________________?
Could you ______________________________?

Unit 7

astronaut

camel

Christmas

circus

environment

Halloween

mechanic

pyramid

Adjectives

bored / boring

depressed / depressing

embarrassed / embarrassing

excited / exciting

exhausted / exhausting

frightened / frightening

interested / interesting

worried / worrying

Present perfect, affirmative with *for / since*

I / You / We / They **have worked** there **since** 2002.
He / She / It **has been** in that city **for** one month.

1 Read, write, and circle.

1. travel	2. see (*neg.*)	3. be	4. rain	5. blow
6. feel	7. have (*neg.*)	8. eat	9. drink	10. begin

Columbus sailed across the Atlantic Ocean from August 3, 1492, to October 12, 1492.

October 11, 1492

Your Royal Majesties:

The news isn't good. We (1) *have traveled* **for / since** two months, but we (2) ____________ any trace of land yet. The weather (3) ____________ terrible **for / since** almost two weeks. It (4) ____________ heavily and the wind (5) ____________ hard **for / since** yesterday. All of us (6) ____________ seasick **for / since** the bad weather started. We (7) ____________ any supplies **for / since** last month. We (8) ____________ pieces of stale bread and (9) ____________ only a little water in the last three days.

The sailors (10) ____________ to seem worried.

I understand their feeling. It is a worrying situation.

We all hope to find land soon!

Yours sincerely,

Christopher Columbus

Present perfect, negative with *in* / *since*

I / You / We / They **haven't seen** us **in** two years.
He / She / It **hasn't eaten since** yesterday morning.

1 Read and write.

get go play run take wear

1 My last Halloween costume
October 31, 2012

2 Mom's last exercise class
May, last year

3 Ben's last soccer game
2010

4 Sheila's last A+
two weeks ago

5 Their last trip to the circus
November 2014

6 Your last race
six months ago

1. I *haven't worn* a Halloween costume since *2012*.
2. My mom ________________ to an exercise class for ________________.
3. Ben ________________ a game in ________________.
4. Sheila ________________ an A+ for ________________.
5. My parents ________________ me to the circus since ________________.
6. You ________________ a race in ________________.

2 Read and write about yourself.

1. I haven't ______________________________ in ________________.
2. I haven't ______________________________ since ________________.

Present perfect, interrogative with *ever* 19

1 Read and write.

Egypt Tour Questionnaire

1. (*ride*) QUESTION: *Have you ever ridden* a camel? It's bumpy, but it's a lot of fun!
   ANSWER: *No, I haven't*.
2. (*climb*) Q: ______________________ a pyramid? The pyramids of Egypt are famous.
   A: ________________. Once, I visited the Mayan ruins in Yucatán.
3. (*eat*) Q: ______________________ Egyptian food? The meat in pita bread is delicious.
   A: ________________. I'd like to try it one day.
4. (*sail*) Q: ______________________ down a river? A journey down the Nile is amazing!
   A: ________________. I've sailed down the Mississippi.

2 Mark for yourself and write.

✓ = have ✗ = haven't

____ travel to another country ____ see ancient pyramids

____ fly in a plane ____ eat interesting foods

1. *Have you ever traveled to another country*? ____________.
2. ______________________________? ____________.
3. ______________________________? ____________.
4. ______________________________? ____________.

Present perfect with *How long...?*

1 Read and write.

attend be live support

Planet Protectors: The Environmental Magazine for Kids

Protector Profile: Elaine Richards

My name is Elaine Richards. I was born in New York, but I've lived in Sydney for two years. I'm twelve years old, and I've attended secondary school for four months.

I've been a member of Greenpeace since 2013, and I'm very interested in sharing some ideas with you and inviting you to participate in all the organization's projects.

Greenpeace focuses on the most important worldwide threats to our planet's environment. It has been in existence since 1971.

One of Greenpeace's missions is to protect the ancient forests. They want to prevent the species that live there from becoming extinct. They help orangutans in Asia, wolves in North America, tigers in Russia, and jaguars in the Amazon.

For the last few years, children around the world have supported the "Protecting Ancient Forests" campaign. I hope you can join us in helping the environment!

1. How long has Elaine been a member of Greenpeace? Since 2001.
2. How ________ she ________ in Sydney? For ________.
3. ________ she ________ secondary school? ________.
4. ________ Greenpeace ________ in existence? ________.
5. ________ children ________ the forest campaign? ________.

Practice with the Pathway to Certification app!

Adjectives with *-ed/-ing*

1 Read and circle.

1. Tom finds astronomy ***fascinated*** / ***fascinating***.
   He has been ***fascinated*** / ***fascinating*** by the stars since he was very young.
2. Rainy weather is ***depressed*** / ***depressing***. Rainy weather makes me feel ***depressed*** / ***depressing***.
3. The musicians' performance was ***entertained*** / ***entertaining***.
   The audience was very ***entertained*** / ***entertaining*** by their performance.
4. Adam has a ***bored*** / ***boring*** summer job in an office.
   He's very ***bored*** / ***boring*** because he doesn't have much work to do.

2 Read, write, and number.

amazing   embarrassing   exhausted   frightening   interested

1

1. Last Saturday, my family and I went to the circus. All the acts were amazing!
2. My sister thought the wire tricks were a little ________________. They were so high in the air!
3. My cousins were really ________________ in the acrobats' performance.
4. My dad was called onstage during the clown act. It was funny, but so ________________!
5. We all enjoyed the show and got home ________________.

3 Read and write.

shocked bored disgusting entertaining frightened interesting

Maggie hasn't had a party since last year. Why?

Last October, Maggie had a Halloween party. Everyone wore *interesting* costumes. Her friends gave her a present. But she was really ______________ when she opened it! It looked like a big, scary spider!

Last December, Maggie had a Christmas party. She asked a band to play Christmas carols. She thought their music would be ______________. But they played the same songs over and over again, so everyone was ______________. Lots of people left early.

On New Year's Eve, Maggie threw another party. It was fun, but at the end of the party, her house was so dirty that it looked ______________. Maggie and her parents were ______________ at the mess. It took them hours to clean the house! They said, "No more parties!"

4 Write and draw.

Write a story about a party. Use the *–ed* and *–ing* forms of adjectives.

I've had many parties at my house, but this one was different.

____

____

____

____

5 Follow and write.

astronaut chef firefighter mechanic pilot scientist

1. Dad
2. Grandpa
3. Mom
4. My cousins
5. Aunt June
6. Uncle Henry

fight fires
cook in a restaurant
fly planes
fix cars
be interested in science
be fascinated by the stars

2002
15 years
1980
6 months
the last 25 years
10 years

1. How long has Dad flown planes ?
   He's flown planes for the last 25 years . He's a pilot .
2. How long ____________________ ?
   ____________________ . He's a ________ .
3. ____________________ ?
   ____________________ . ________ .
4. ____________________ ?
   ____________________ . ________ .
5. ____________________ ?
   ____________________ . ________ .
6. ____________________ ?
   ____________________ . ________ .

6 Read and write about yourself.

My Hobby, My Career

I've been interested in ____________ ***for / since*** ____________ .

I want to be ***a / an*** ____________ someday.

1 Listen and label the pictures. 20

AMANDA: We all have different abilities. Angela, what are you good at?

ANGELA: I'm good at dancing. I've always been fascinated with ballet, tap, and folkloric dances. I've taken a lot of classes, and I've practiced dance for many years. Are you good at dancing, Amanda?

AMANDA: No, I'm not. I haven't danced since New Year's Eve, 2013! That was the night I danced and danced, and then I slipped and fell down. Everyone laughed, and I was so embarrassed!

ANGELA: I'm sure you're good at other things, though.

AMANDA: Well, I'm good at math. Some people think math is boring, but I've been interested in numbers since I was a little kid. There are lots of ways to apply math in real life. It's exciting!

ANGELA: Maybe you could help me with math sometime.

AMANDA: And maybe you could teach me to dance!

____

____

2 Read the dialogue with a friend.

3 Talk with a friend. Then write.

Adjectives

embarrassed	excited	fascinated	frightened	interested
embarrassing	exciting	fascinating	frightening	interesting

A: What are you good at?

B: I'm good at ________________. I've been interested in ________________ for / since ________________.

A: Is there anything you aren't good at?

B: I'm not good at ________________.

It's / I'm ____________________________.
(adjective)

How about you? What are you good at?

Let's sing!

1 Read and complete. Then, listen and check. 21

How Long?

How long have you had (*have*) that pen?
I ______________ (*have*) it for two weeks.
Look, I got it from my favorite store.
The problem is it leaks.

Chorus:
For several months, since I __________ (*see*) Elvis once.
For one long hour, since I __________ (*take*) my shower.

How long __________ you __________ (*have*) that ring?
I've had it since last June.
My brother __________ (*buy*) it for my birthday.
Great! It's my birthday again soon!

(Chorus)

How long __________ you __________ (*have*) that book?
It's new, since half past two.
I __________ already __________ (*read*) most of it.
When I'm done, I'll lend it to you.

(Chorus)

How long __________ you __________ (*have*) that bike?
I ______________ (*have*) it for years.
For a long time, I __________ (*be*) scared to ride.
But now, I don't have any fears.

(Chorus)

Unit 8

belt

castle

crown

queen

channels

graduate (*v*)

join (*v*)

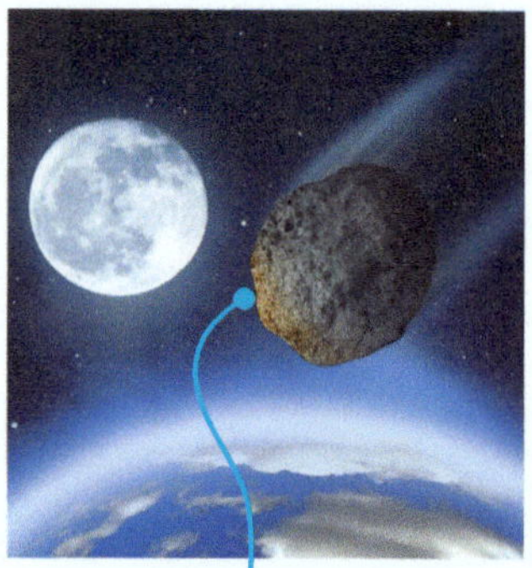

meteor

necklace

pocket

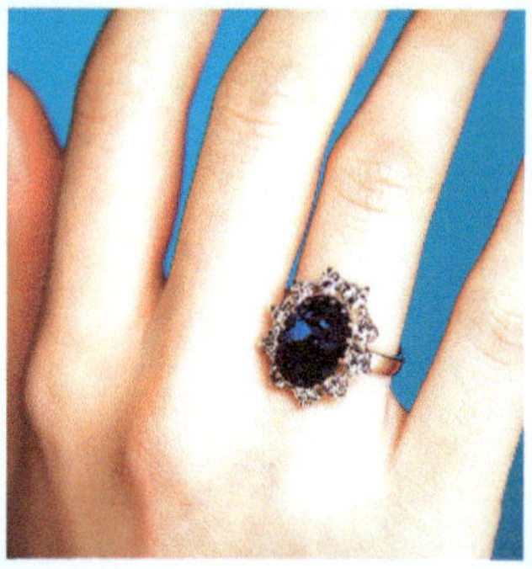

ring

roller coaster

slippery (*adj*)

storm (*n*) / stormy (*adj*)

town

wild (*adj*)

Simple future, affirmative and negative

I / You / He / She / It / We / They'll sleep in the car.
I / You / He / She / It / We / They won't be awake.

1 Read and match.

1. Monday: icy	The roads will be slippery and dangerous.
2. Tuesday: stormy	It will be very windy!
3. Wednesday: foggy	People won't be able to see very far.
4. Thursday: snowy	You'll need your sunglasses.
5. Friday: sunny	Some of the roads won't be open.

2 Draw and write about yourself.

Tomorrow, the weather in my town will be

______________________________.

I'll wear ______________________________.

I won't wear ______________________________.

✓ ✗

3 Write about yourself. Use *will* and *won't*.

What will you do when you graduate from school?

____

____.

Simple future, interrogative 22

1 Unscramble, look, and write.

1. weather / rainy / the / be / tomorrow / will

   Will the weather be rainy tomorrow?

   Yes, it will. Mary won't go to the beach.

2. to the ceremony / the / wear / a necklace / will / queen

   ______________________________?

   No, she won't, but she __________ the royal crown and a ring.

3. a meteor / the Earth / travel / will / near

   ______________________________?

   ______________, but it __________ hit our planet.

4. will / people / concert / a lot of / go to / the

   ______________________________?

   ______________, so my parents __________ buy tickets online early.

5. return / Mom / tomorrow / will / and Dad

   ______________________________?

   ______________. They __________ be back until next Friday.

Modal verbs *may, might*

1 Look and write.

may may not might might not

1. Bring your sunglasses. It __might__ be sunny this afternoon—you never know!
2. It's cold! Don't forget your jacket, or you ________________ be warm enough.
3. Do you have a scarf? It isn't windy now, but you ________________ need it later.
4. Don't forget gloves. You ________________ have to put your hands in your pockets, too.

2 Look, read, and circle.

1. You ***may*** / ***may not*** need your umbrella. Otherwise, you ***might*** / ***might not*** get wet!
2. Dad ***may*** / ***may not*** need a belt. His jeans ***might*** / ***might not*** be the right size.
3. Customers ***may*** / ***may not*** like rings. They ***might*** / ***might not*** like necklaces better.
4. I ***might*** / ***might not*** have a hole in my pocket. I ***may*** / ***may not*** lose money if I keep it there!

Question words with *might*

1 Read and match.

1. When might we go to the mountains?
2. Where might she find a good recipe?
3. What might they do in our town this weekend?
4. Which book might he read next?
5. How might people get to the theater?

A mystery by Agatha Christie.
By walking.
Go to the movies.
In her grandmother's cookbook.
The first day it snows.

2 Look, read, and write.

1. What might the farmer do later?
   He might feed the animals.

2. What might the girls do next?
   ______________________________.

3. Where might Mom go today?
   ______________________________.

4. What might the story be about?
   ______________________________.

Verb + infinitive

1 Read and circle the infinitives.

Ivan's mom was in a storm. She's describing her experience:

I agreed (to drive) a friend home. After I dropped her off, there was a terrible storm. A tree fell on the road and blocked my way! I needed to turn around. I expected to find my way back to town easily, but I got lost. I drove around for hours. I started to feel worried, so I stopped to ask for directions. I'm glad I did!

2 Read and write.

become bring develop help interview know prepare prevent watch use

Meet Our New Weather Forecaster!

Have you ever forgotten to bring your umbrella and been caught in the rain later? That's what forecaster Stacy Cabrillo wants ______________. We asked some students ______________ Ms. Cabrillo. Remember ______________ her every morning at 6 a.m.!

Students:

When did you decide ______________ a weather forecaster?

How do you hope ______________ your TV viewers?

What technology do you expect ______________ for forecasting in the future?

Ms. Cabrillo:

When I was a kid, I wanted ______________ which clothes to wear for the weather!

I'd love ______________ my TV viewers for their day at work or school.

We're just beginning ______________ new satellite and radar technology.

Verb + gerund

1 Look, match, and write.

1. Agnes didn't practice
2. Paul suggested
3. Elsa's little brother won't stop
4. James told Anna, "I can't help
5. Edgar's mother wants him to finish
6. The dog misses

changing the channel.
doing his homework.
falling in love with you."
following her around everywhere.
going on walks with his owner.
singing before her performance.

1. Agnes didn't practice singing before her performance.
2. ______.
3. ______.
4. ______.
5. ______.
6. ______.

2 Read and write.

may may not might might not will won't

From: uncle.rick@imail.com

To: henry.2014@imail.com

Subject: Camping trip!

Hi Henry,

Are you ready for our camping trip? This is the plan. We will drive up to the forest in the morning. The weather forecast says that it definitely __________ rain on Saturday afternoon, so we'll have good weather when we hike to the campsite!

We'll probably eat at the campsite when we arrive. But there's a small chance that we __________ stop and have lunch along the way. I think it's more likely that we __________ have enough time.

Here's a nice surprise: your cousin Andy __________ join us on the trip. He's free this weekend. Please call him to convince him to come! He __________ bring his guitar because it's so heavy. But we'll need music! Could you bring your harmonica?

See you soon,

Uncle Rick

3 Read and circle.

From: uncle.rick@imail.com

To: henry.2014@imail.com

Subject: Re: Camping trip!

P.S. I can't help ***to give*** / ***giving*** you some tips, since this is your first time camping!

I suggest ***to make*** / ***making*** a list so you don't forget anything.

1. It won't be rainy, so you won't need ***to take*** / ***taking*** an umbrella or a jacket.
2. Remember ***to wear*** / ***wearing*** hiking boots. They will protect your feet on hikes.
3. Don't forget ***to pick up*** / ***picking up*** trash so you don't attract wild animals!
4. Plan ***to bring*** / ***bring*** a first aid kit in case of any emergencies.

You'll love ***to camp*** / ***camping***! I'm sure we'll have a great time.

Let's talk!

1 Listen and write. 23

DOUG: This school club fair is enormous! What are you planning __________? I see __________ clubs, the __________ Club, the Chess Club, and the Multicultural Club.

CINDY: Well, I don't like __________ very much. I prefer __________ and dancing. I may join the __________ Club!

DOUG: I'm just the opposite. I don't like singing and dancing, but I love __________ __________ and tennis! I may join some __________ clubs.

CINDY: What about the Multicultural Club?

DOUG: That club might be the most __________. I've heard that they have dinners where everyone brings __________ from different __________!

CINDY: I might __________ the Multicultural Club, too, then.

DOUG: Me, too!

School Club Fair Today!

Sports Clubs
Tennis • Basketball
Baseball • Soccer

Theater Club
Sing • Act
Dance

Chess Club
Learn • Practice
Win

Multicultural Club
Learn languages
Enjoy cultural foods

2 Read the dialogue with a friend.

3 Talk with a friend. Then write.

A: What activities do you like doing?

B: I like __________. I prefer __________ to __________. I don't like __________.

A: I think you should join the __________ Club!

B: You're right! / No, I prefer the __________ club. What activities do you like doing?

Zero conditional	
condition (present)	**result (present)**
If you water plants every day,	they grow.
If you don't put them in the sun,	they don't grow.
result (present)	**condition (present)**
Plants grow	**if** you water them every day.
Plants don't grow	**if** you don't put them in the sun.

Problem verbs			
borrow (from someone)	lend (to someone)	earn (a salary)	win (a prize, the lottery)
lose (an object)	miss (an opportunity)	meet (for the first time)	know (for a period of time)

Make		*Do*	
your bed	food	an activity	exercise
a decision	a mistake	chores	laundry
dinner	a phone call	homework	a puzzle

Too, not … enough

These jeans are too big.

These jeans aren't big enough.

Unit 3

Used to	
What did Grandpa use to do?	He used to ride his bike to work. He didn't use to take the bus.

Unit 4

Prepositions of movement		
across	along	down
into	onto	over
past	through	toward
up		

Passive voice in past, affirmative		
I	was	taken to the hospital. seen by other people. sung by Rihanna. written by Shakespeare. discovered by Columbus.
You	were	
He / She It*	was	
We / You They*	were	

*most common forms

Passive voice in past, interrogative			
Was	I	given a present? painted by Da Vinci? hit by an iceberg? stolen by robbers?	Yes, you were. / No, you weren't.
Were	you		Yes, I was. / No, I wasn't.
Was	he / she it*		Yes, he / she was. / No, he / she wasn't. Yes, it was.* / No, it wasn't.*
Were	we / you they*		Yes, you / we were. / No, you / we weren't. Yes, they were.* / No, they weren't.*

*most common forms

Unit 5

First conditional	
condition (present)	**result (future)**
If it's hot outside,	I'll wear shorts.
If it's not windy,	we won't fly a kite.
Unless* the rain stops,	we won't go bike riding.
result (future)	**condition (present)**
We'll eat at good restaurants	**if** we go to the city.
They'll lose the game	**if** he doesn't wear his lucky sock.
You won't get a good grade	**unless*** you study hard.

*unless = the result will happen if the condition *doesn't* happen or *isn't* true

Need to	
You need to do your homework.	You don't need to bring a jacket.
You don't need to be handsome to be a movie star.	

Unit 6

Offers with *would*	
Would you like to do a puzzle? Yes, I would. / No, I wouldn't.	What would you like to order? I'll have the chicken, please.

Requests with *could*	
Could you buy me a newspaper?	Could we have two tickets, please?

Present perfect, affirmative				
I	have	(I've)	(already)	bought a gift. taken a nap. waited in line. eaten lunch.
You		(You've)		
He She It	has	(He's) (She's) (It's)		
We You They	have	(We've) (You've) (They've)		

Present perfect, negative					
I	have	not	(I haven't)	washed the dishes fed the dog gone to Europe taken a shower	(yet).
You			(You haven't)		
He She It	has		(He hasn't) (She hasn't) (It hasn't)		
We You They	have		(We haven't) (You haven't) (They haven't)		

Present perfect, interrogative				
Have	I	gone swimming met my cousin added flour tasted the soup	(yet)?	Yes, you have. / No, you haven't.
	you			Yes, I have. / No, I haven't.
Has	he she it			Yes, he has. / No, he hasn't. Yes, she has. / No, she hasn't. Yes, it has. / No, it hasn't.
Have	we you they			Yes, you have. / No, you haven't. Yes, we have. / No, we haven't. Yes, they have. / No, they haven't.

Present perfect, negative with *in, since*	
She hasn't been to the doctor **in** a year.	We haven't gone to the movies **since** October.

Present perfect with *How long, for, since*	
How long have you lived here?	I've lived here **for** ten years. I've lived here **since** 2015.

Present perfect, interrogative with *ever*	
Have you **ever** gone snorkeling?	Yes, I have. / No, I haven't.

Adjectives ending in *–ed, –ing*			
He's **interested** in science.		He thinks science is **interesting**.	
depressed	depressing	fascinated	fascinating
bored	boring	entertained	entertaining
amazed	amazing	embarrassed	embarrassing
exhausted	exhausting	frightened	frightening
interested	interesting	disgusted	disgusting
excited	exciting		

Modal verbs *may, might*, affirmative and negative			
I You He She It We You They	may might	(not)	be rainy tomorrow. call a doctor. travel to Brazil. lend you a book.

Verb + infinitive He wants to dance.		Verb + Gerund or Infinitive	Verb + gerund She stopped dancing.	
agree	hope	begin	can't help	stop
decide	need	like	finish	suggest
expect	remember	love	miss	
forget	want	start	practice	
have			quit	

Irregular Verb Forms					
Base Form	**Past**	**Past Participle**	**Base Form**	**Past**	**Past Participle**
become	became	become	feel	felt	felt
begin	began	begun	fight	fought	fought
blow	blew	blown	find	found	found
break	broke	broken	fly	flew	flown
bring	brought	brought	forbid	forbid	forbidden
build	built	built	forget	forgot	forgotten
buy	bought	bought	get	got	gotten
come	came	come	give	gave	given
cut	cut	cut	go	went	gone
do	did	done	grow	grew	grown
drink	drank	drunk	have	had	had
drive	drove	driven	hear	heard	heard
eat	ate	eaten	hide	hid	hidden
fall	fell	fallen	hold	held	held
feed	fed	fed	know	knew	known

Irregular Verb Forms					
Base Form	**Past**	**Past Participle**	**Base Form**	**Past**	**Past Participle**
leave	left	left	sing	sang	sung
lend	lent	lent	sink	sank	sunk
lie	lay	laid	sleep	slept	slept
lose	lost	lost	spend	spent	spent
make	made	made	steal	stole	stolen
meet	met	met	swim	swam	swum
put	put	put	take	took	taken
quit	quit	quit	teach	taught	taught
read	read	read	think	thought	thought
ride	rode	ridden	throw	threw	thrown
run	ran	run	wear	wore	worn
see	saw	seen	win	won	won
sell	sold	sold	write	wrote	written
send	sent	sent			

Audio script

Unit 1

Track 1

WOLF: I'm going to get you, three little kittens! I'll huff, and I'll puff, and I'll blow your house down!
KITTEN 1: Oh, no! My house is made of paper!
KITTEN 2: Oh, no! My house is made of wood!
KITTEN 3: You can't scare me! My house is made of metal! Goodbye, Mr. Wolf!

Track 2

HARRY: That box is heavy, isn't it?
EMMA: Yes, it is! Can you help me pick it up?
HARRY: Sure! It goes in the kitchen, doesn't it?
EMMA: Yes, but let's be careful. The box is made of paper, and there are heavy plates inside!
HARRY: It's okay. The plates are made of plastic, aren't they?
EMMA: No, they aren't!
HARRY: Oops.
EMMA: Oh, no! All the plates are broken!
HARRY: Mom isn't going to be happy about this, is she?
EMMA: No, she isn't.

Track 3

The Empty Room

(See page 13.)

Unit 2

Track 4

GARDENER: See? Gardening isn't difficult. If you water plants every day, they grow.
ASSISTANT: What's this plant?
GARDENER: It's a carnivorous plant. It eats meat!
ASSISTANT: Uh… What?
GARDENER: Go ahead. Feed it a little meat.
ASSISTANT: Okay… Ouch!
GARDENER: Oh, I forgot to tell you! If you don't feed carnivorous plants carefully, they bite!

Track 5

MOM: Would you like to learn how to make peanut butter cookies?
MIKE: Yes, I would! What should I do first?
MOM: First, mix a cup of peanut butter, a cup of sugar, a teaspoon of vanilla, and an egg in a bowl.
DAD: Next, drop spoonfuls of the mixture onto a baking sheet.
MOM: If you use a fork to make cross marks, the cookies look pretty.
DAD: Then, bake the cookies for ten minutes.
MOM: Be careful. If you bake cookies too long, they burn!
DAD: Finally, let the cookies cool.
MOM: If cookies don't have time to cool, they get too soft.
MIKE: Thanks, Mom and Dad! These cookies are delicious!

Track 6

Extreme Sports

Do you want to go snowboarding today?
If you do, get your board and follow me.
Put your helmet on and balance.
Let yourself go and fly through the air.

Do you feel the spray of snow on your face?
Don't let the snow beat you.

Chorus:
Extreme sports, extreme sports
I'd like to do them all.
They're frightening; I'm scared.
They're exciting and fun.
They're not boring at all!

Do you want to go whitewater rafting today?
If you do, get your raft and follow me.
Put your life jacket on. We're off!
Take your seat and paddle down the rapids.

Do you feel the spray of water on your face?
Don't let the speed beat you.

(Chorus)

Unit 3

Track 7

BOY 1: This morning, we went to the beach, but the waves looked big and dangerous!
BOY 2: We didn't surf. We didn't swim in the ocean.
GIRL: We went home and now we're swimming in the pool!

Track 8

DAVID: Hi, Holly! How was your vacation?
HOLLY: Hi, David! Spain was beautiful, but I'm glad to be home!
DAVID: Why? What happened?
HOLLY: First, we flew to Madrid. The flight was great. But the airline lost our suitcases!
DAVID: Oh, no! What did you do next?
HOLLY: Next, we went shopping in the city. We had to buy all new clothes!
DAVID: What happened then?
HOLLY: Then, my dad lost his credit card.
DAVID: Did he find it?
HOLLY: No, he didn't! Finally, we went to Bilbao to see the Guggenheim Museum.
DAVID: That place is amazing, isn't it?
HOLLY: I don't know. On the day we went, it was closed!

Track 9

My Lady

Chorus:
Where did you go, my lady?
Why are you so far from me?
When can I see you, my lady?
You know I need you,
I need you with me!

I played a million games,
I went a thousand miles,
I watched a hundred faces,
Just to see you smile

(Chorus)

Not the highest mountain,
Not the biggest sea,
Not the longest river,
Can keep you from me!

Unit 4

Track 10

BOY: Is your house very far away?
GIRL: No, it's easy to get to my house! Just follow my directions.
BOY: Okay.
GIRL: Just go along the path… through the trees… across the bridge… down the hill… and up the stairs!
BOY: Whew!

Track 11

DANNY: Wow, I can't believe we're finally at the Olympics!
SARAH: Yes, but I think we're late! Excuse me, what time does the opening ceremony start?
GUIDE: It starts at 7 p.m. You'd better hurry!
SARAH: Sorry, what time? Could you say that again, please?
GUIDE: Seven o'clock.
DANNY: Can you tell us how to get there?
GUIDE: Go along this path toward the stadium. Walk through the gate and up the stairs. Then, just show the guards your tickets.
DANNY: Thank you!
GUIDE: Have a great time at the ceremony!

Track 12

Summer Camp

Last week I went to the lake.
I camped under the stars,
And played with a snake.
I hiked up the mountain,
And painted a fountain, ooh!

Chorus:
It's because I went to summer camp,
Summer camp, playing in the sun.
Summer camp, summer camp:
Games, friends and lots of fun.
Summer camp, summer camp,
I went to summer camp.

I sailed on a boat at sea.
I walked up and down the beach,
And climbed up a great palm tree.
I surfed on really big waves,
And visited some interesting caves, ooh!

(Chorus)

Summer camp, summer camp,
Summer camp, playing in the sun.
Summer camp, summer camp:
Games, friends and lots of fun.
Summer camp, summer camp,
I went to summer camp!

Unit 5

Track 13

GIRL 1: I like the new boy in school.
GIRL 2: What's he like?
GIRL 1: He's really cute. If I see him tomorrow, I'll invite him to my party!
GIRL 2: Look, there he is!
GIRL 1: Hi Brad! My birthday is this weekend. Can you come to my party on Sunday?
BOY: Uh… Sure, I guess so.
GIRL 1: See? He's so cute!
GIRL 2: Hmm… If he actually comes to your party, I'll be really surprised!

Track 14

FEMALE NURSE: Good morning, City hospital. How can I help you?
MALE PATIENT: I think I need to see a doctor right away!
NURSE: What's the matter?
PATIENT: Well, I didn't brush my teeth last night.
NURSE: If you have a toothache, you'll need to see a dentist, not a doctor.
PATIENT: No, I don't have a toothache.
NURSE: What's the matter, then?
PATIENT: It's my toes and my finger. I got out of bed to brush my teeth. It was dark, so I didn't see a toy on the floor. I fell down and hurt my toes. I cut my finger, too!
NURSE: Okay. I don't think we need to send an ambulance, but you need to see the doctor in his office. I'll tell him you're coming.
PATIENT: Thank you! Good-bye.
NURSE: Good-bye.

Track 15

When I Was a Little Kid

Chorus:
When I was a little kid,
I didn't do a lot of things.
How could I be such a fool?
When I was a little kid,
I didn't do a lot of things.
What a waste of time!

I didn't like to eat fish then.
My mom tried and tried for hours.
I didn't like to eat fish then.
But I kept my mouth closed tight!

(Chorus)
I didn't like to dance at all.
I only watched kids having fun.
I didn't like to dance at all,
All by myself drinking juice!

(Chorus)

I didn't ride my bike to the park.
I didn't play with other kids.
I didn't ride my bike to the park,
So I watched TV and got fat!

(Chorus)

Unit 6

Track 16

WAITER: Your lunch is served. Would you like some pepper on your salad, sir?
DINER: Yes, please.
DINER: *Ah-Ah-ACHOO!*
WAITER: Sir? Would you like a tissue?
DINER: No, no, just the check, thanks.

Track 17

ROSA: Mike, would you like to eat at a restaurant tonight?
MIKE: Sure, Aunt Rosa!
ROSA: Where would you like to go?
MIKE: How about the Argentinian restaurant?
ROSA: I'm sorry. I can't eat a lot of meat. What about the French bakery? They have great desserts!
MIKE: I don't like eating too much sugar. Could we try another place?
ROSA: What about the new Italian restaurant?
MIKE: That's a good idea. I haven't eaten there yet! Could you drive us?
ROSA: Yes, I can. I've already got my car keys!

Track 18

Could You Do Me a Favor?

(See page 63.)

Unit 7

Track 19

GUIDE: Welcome to your African safari! There are many amazing animals here on the savannah. Have you ever seen a lion?
TOURISTS: Yes, we have! / Sure. / Well, yeah.
One tourist: But only in a zoo! Usually, the lions are asleep.
GUIDE: Well, today, you can see a lion awake and in the wild. There's one right there! Uh oh, he's looking right at us. Have you ever heard a lion's roar?
TOURISTS: No, we haven't!
GUIDE: Now you have!

Track 20

(See page 72.)

Track 21

How Long?

How long have you had that pen?
I've had it for two weeks.
Look, I got it from my favorite store.
The problem is it leaks.

Chorus:
For several months,
Since I saw Elvis once.
For one long hour,
Since I took my shower.

How long have you had that ring?
I've had it since last June.
My brother bought it for my birthday.
Great! It's my birthday again soon!

(Chorus)

How long have you had that book?
It's new, since half past two.
I've already read most of it.
When I'm done I'll lend it to you.

(Chorus)

How long have you had that bike?
I've had it for years.
For a long time, I was scared to ride.
But now, I don't have any fears.

(Chorus)

Unit 8

Track 22

BOY 1: Will I really like riding the roller coaster? It looks so tall and fast!
BOY 2: Yes, you will! This is the most exciting roller coaster I've ever ridden!
Ride attendant: Please step into the car and fasten your safety belt carefully!
BOY 1: Uh oh… I don't feel very good. Will I be sick?
BOY 2: No, you won't! Just try to enjoy it. Wheeeeee!

Track 23

DOUG: This school club fair is enormous! What are you planning to join? I see sports clubs, the Theater Club, the Chess Club, and a Multicultural Club.
CINDY: Well, I don't like playing sports very much. I prefer singing and dancing. I may join the Theater Club!
DOUG: I'm just the opposite. I don't like singing and dancing, but I love playing soccer and tennis! I may join some sports clubs.
CINDY: What about the Multicultural Club?
DOUG: That club might be the most fun. I've heard that they have dinners where everyone brings food from different countries!
CINDY: I might join the Multicultural Club, too, then.
DOUG: Me, too!

Track 24

What Might We Find?

We're going on an adventure.
What might we find?
We might find a big castle,
With a green dragon inside.

We're going to hunt for treasure.
What might we find?
We might find an old trunk,
With gold and silver inside.

We're going swimming and diving.
What might we see?
We might see colored rocks,
At the bottom of the sea.

We're flying in a red balloon.
What might we do?
We might fly really fast,
And say good-bye to you!

Vocabulary